We would like to hear from you. Please send your comments
about this book to us in care of zreview@zondervan.com. Thank you.

ZONDERVAN

Jesus

Copyright © 2010 by Philip D. Yancey and SCCT

Text based on *The Jesus I Never Knew*

Copyright © 1995 by Philip D. Yancey and SCCT

This title is also available as a Zondervan ebook. Visit www.zondervan.com/ebooks.

Requests for information should be addressed to:

Zondervan, *Grand Rapids, Michigan 49530*

ISBN 978-0-310-29320-0

Creative direction and design by Mark Arnold, andArnold Books.

Printed in the United States of America

10 11 12 13 14 /SBM/ 20 19 18 17 16 15 14 13 12 11 10 9 8 7 6 5 4 3 2 1

JESUS

Philip Yancey

creative direction by
mark arnold

andArnold books

The Word was first,
  the Word present to God,
  God present to the Word.

The Word was God.

Everything was created through him;
  nothing—not one thing!—
  came into being without him.

What came into existence was Life,
  and the Life was Light to live by.
The Life-Light blazed out of the darkness;
  the darkness couldn't put it out.

He came to his own people,
  but they didn't want him.

But whoever did want him,
  who believed he was who he claimed
  and would do what he said,
He made to be their true selves,
  their child-of-God selves.

These are the God-begotten,
  not blood-begotten,
  not flesh-begotten,
  not sex-begotten.

The word became flesh and blood, and
MOVED INTO
the

NEIGHBOR-
HOOD.

ICONS OF THE ORTHODOX CHURCH, STAINED-GLASS WINDOWS IN EUROPEAN CATHEDRALS, AND SUNDAY SCHOOL ART IN LOW-CHURCH AMERICA ALL DEPICT ON FLAT PLANES A PLACID, "TAME" JESUS, YET THE JESUS I MET IN THE GOSPELS WAS ANYTHING BUT TAME. HIS SEARING

HONESTY MADE HIM SEEM DOWNRIGHT TACTLESS IN SOME SETTINGS. FEW PEOPLE FELT COMFORTABLE AROUND HIM; THOSE WHO DID WERE THE TYPE NO ONE ELSE FELT COMFORTABLE AROUND. HE WAS NOTORIOUSLY DIFFICULT TO PREDICT, PIN DOWN, OR EVEN UNDERSTAND.

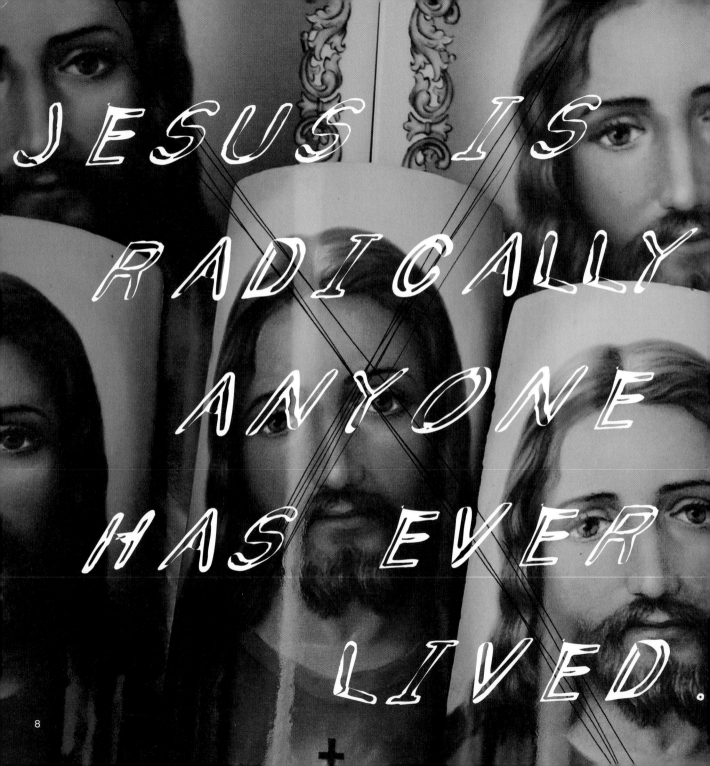

JESUS IS RADICALLY ANYONE HAS EVER LIVED.

UNLIKE

ELSE WHO

TWO WORDS ONE COULD NEVER
THINK OF APPLYING TO THE JESUS
OF THE GOSPELS: BORING
AND PREDICTABLE.

THE JESUS OF

IS THE BEST-KE

CHRISTIANITY.

THE GOSPELS
PT SECRET OF

The God who roared, who could order armies and empires about like pawns on a chessboard, this God emerged in Palestine as a

baby who could not speak or eat solid food or control his own bladder, who

depended on a teenager for shelter, food, and love.

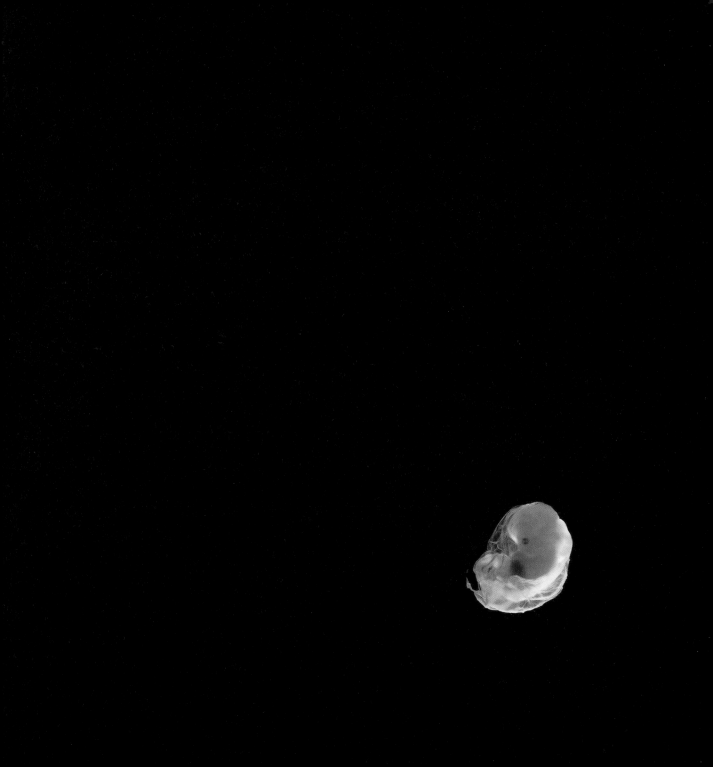

IN THE MODERN UNITED STATES, where each year a million teenage girls get pregnant out of wedlock, Mary's predicament has undoubtedly lost some of its force, but in a closely knit Jewish community in the first century, the news an angel brought could not have been entirely welcome. The law regarded a betrothed woman who became pregnant as an adulteress, subject to death by stoning.

Today as I read the accounts of Jesus' birth

I tremble to think of the fate of the world resting on the responses of two rural teenagers. How many times did Mary review the angel's words as she felt the Son of God kicking against the walls of her uterus? How many times did Joseph second-guess his own encounter with an angel—just a dream?—as he endured the hot shame of living among villagers who could plainly see the changing shape of his fiancée?

THE BURNING BUSH OF MOSES, the hot coals of Isaiah, the extraterrestrial visions of Ezekiel—a person "blessed" with a direct encounter with God expected to come away scorched or glowing or maybe half-crippled like Jacob. These were the fortunate ones: Jewish children also learned stories of the sacred mountain in the desert that proved fatal to everyone who touched it. Mishandle the ark of the covenant, and you died. Enter the Most Holy Place, and you'd never come out alive. Among people who walled off a separate sanctum for God in the temple and shrank from pronouncing or spelling out the name, God made a surprise appearance as a baby in a manger.

What can be less scary than a newborn with his limbs wrapped tight against his body? In Jesus, God found a way of relating to human beings that did not involve fear.

15

JESUS IS MORE:

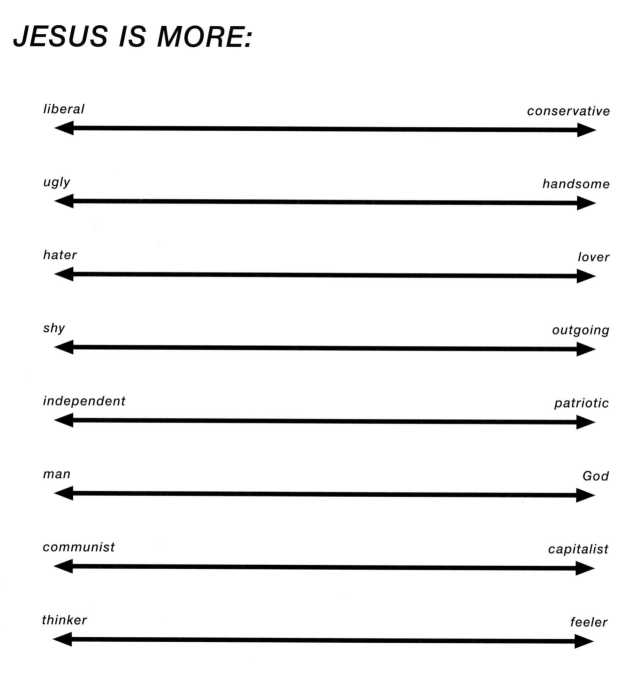

liberal ←————————————————————→ conservative

ugly ←————————————————————→ handsome

hater ←————————————————————→ lover

shy ←————————————————————→ outgoing

independent ←————————————————————→ patriotic

man ←————————————————————→ God

communist ←————————————————————→ capitalist

thinker ←————————————————————→ feeler

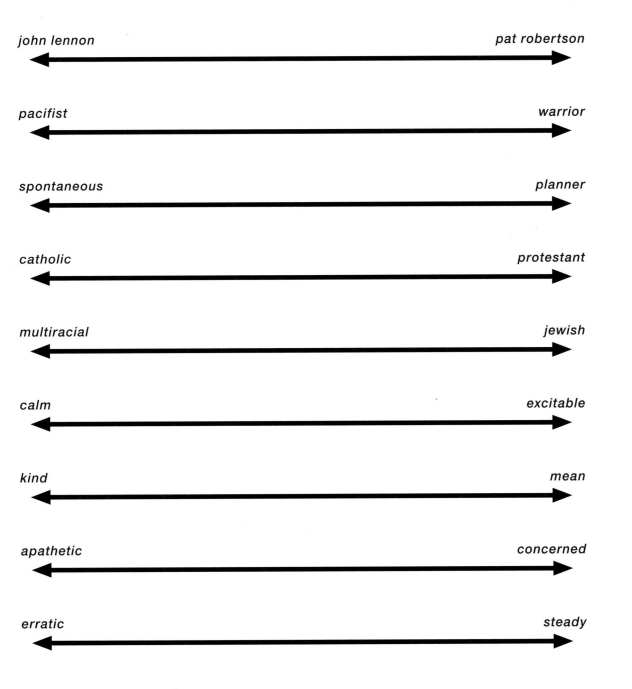

john lennon ←——————————————→ pat robertson

pacifist ←——————————————→ warrior

spontaneous ←——————————————→ planner

catholic ←——————————————→ protestant

multiracial ←——————————————→ jewish

calm ←——————————————→ excitable

kind ←——————————————→ mean

apathetic ←——————————————→ concerned

erratic ←——————————————→ steady

Jesus' audacious claims about himself pose what may be the central problem of all history, the dividing point between Christianity and other religions. Although Muslims and, increasingly, Jews respect Jesus as a great teacher and prophet, no Muslim can imagine Mohammed claiming to be Allah any more than a Jew can imagine Moses claiming to be Yahweh. Likewise, Hindus believe in many incarnations but not one Incarnation, while Buddhists have no categories in which to conceive of a sovereign God becoming a human being.

Jesus' entire life stands or falls on his claim to be God. I cannot trust his promised forgiveness unless he has the authority to back up such an offer. I cannot trust his words about the other side ("I go to prepare a place for you . . .") unless I believe what he said about having come from the Father and returning to the Father. Most important, unless he was in some way God, I must view the cross as an act of divine cruelty rather than sacrificial love.

THE JESUS I LEARNED ABOUT AS A CHILD WAS SWEET AND INOFFENSIVE, THE KIND OF PERSON WHOSE LAP YOU WANT TO CLIMB ONTO. INDEED JESUS DID HAVE QUALITIES OF GENTLENESS AND COMPASSION THAT ATTRACTED CHILDREN. MISTER ROGERS, HOWEVER, HE ASSUREDLY WAS NOT. // IN ALL THE MOVIES MADE ABOUT JESUS' LIFE, SURELY THE MOST PROVOCATIVE – AND PERHAPS THE MOST ACCURATE – PORTRAYAL OF THE SERMON ON THE MOUNT APPEARS IN A LOW-BUDGET BBC PRODUCTION ENTITLED SON OF MAN. ROMAN SOLDIERS HAVE JUST INVADED A GALILEAN VILLAGE TO EXACT VENGEANCE FOR SOME TRESPASS AGAINST THE EMPIRE. THEY HAVE STRUNG UP JEWISH MEN OF FIGHTING AGE, SHOVED THEIR HYSTERICAL WIVES TO THE GROUND, EVEN SPEARED BABIES. INTO THAT TUMULTUOUS SCENE OF **BLOOD AND TEARS** STRIDES JESUS WITH EYES ABLAZE. "I TELL YOU: LOVE YOUR ENEMIES AND PRAY FOR THOSE THAT PERSECUTE YOU," HE SHOUTS ABOVE THE GROANS. YOU CAN IMAGINE THE VILLAGERS' RESPONSE TO SUCH UNWELCOME ADVICE. THE SERMON ON THE MOUNT DID NOT SOOTHE THEM; IT INFURIATED THEM. // IN MY STUDIES I ENCOUNTERED A TERRIFYING ASPECT OF JESUS, ONE THAT I NEVER LEARNED ABOUT IN SUNDAY SCHOOL. THE JESUS I MET IN THE GOSPELS WAS ANYTHING BUT TAME.

The Gospels present a man who has such charisma that people will sit three days straight, without food, just to hear his riveting words. He seems excitable, impulsively "moved with compassion" or "filled with pity." The Gospels reveal a range of Jesus' emotional responses: sudden sympathy for a person with leprosy, exuberance over his disciples' successes, a blast of anger at cold-hearted legalists, grief over an unreceptive city, and then those awful cries of anguish in Gethsemane and on the cross. He had nearly in-exhaust-ible patience with individuals but no patience at all with institutions and injustice.

Three times, at least, he cried in front of his disciples. He did not hide his fears or hesitate to ask for help: "My soul is overwhelmed with sorrow to the point of death," he told them in Gethsemane; "Stay here and keep watch with me."

Jesus, I found, bore little resemblance to the Mister Rogers figure I had met in Sunday school, and was remarkably unlike the person I had studied in Bible college. For one thing, he was far less tame. In my prior image, I realized, Jesus' personality matched that of a Star Trek Vulcan: he remained calm, cool, and collected as he strode like a robot among excitable human beings on spaceship earth. That is not what I found portrayed in the Gospels. Other people affected Jesus deeply: obstinacy frustrated him, self-righteousness infuriated him, simple faith thrilled him. INDEED, HE SEEMED MORE EMOTIONAL AND SPONTANEOUS THAN THE AVERAGE PERSON, NOT LESS. MORE PASSIONATE, NOT LESS.

23

One of Jesus' most scandalous stories is the story of the Good Samaritan. As sentimental as we may have made it, the original story was about a man who gets beat up and left on the side of the road. A priest passes by. A Levite, the quintessential religious guy, also passes by on the other side (perhaps late for a meeting at church). And then comes the Samaritan... you can almost imagine a snicker in the Jewish crowd. Jews did not talk to Samaritans, or even walk through Samaria. But the Samaritan stops and takes care of the guy in the ditch and is lifted up as the hero of the story. I'm sure some of the listeners were ticked. According to the religious elite, Samaritans did not keep the right rules, and they did not have sound doctrine... but Jesus shows that true faith has to work itself out in a way that is Good News to the most bruised and broken person lying in the ditch.

It is so simple, but the pious forget this lesson constantly. God may indeed be evident in a priest,

but God is just as likely to be at work through a Samaritan or a prostitute. In fact the Scripture is brimful of God using folks like a lying prostitute named Rahab, an adulterous king named David... at one point God even speaks to a guy named Balaam through his donkey. So if God should choose to use us, then we should be grateful but not think too highly of ourselves. And if upon meeting someone we think God could never use, we should think again.

After all, Jesus says to the religious elite who looked down on everybody else: "The tax collectors and prostitutes are entering the Kingdom ahead of you." And we wonder what got him killed?

ISRAEL. Gaza. Al Aqsa Martyr Brigades. Militants patrol a side road outside Gaza city in the eventuality of an Israeli incursion.

I have a friend in the UK who talks about "dirty theology" — that we have a God who is always using dirt to bring life and healing and redemption, a God who shows up in the most unlikely and scandalous ways. After all, the whole story begins with God reaching down from heaven, picking up some dirt, and breathing life into it. At one point, Jesus takes some mud, spits in it, and wipes it on a blind man's eyes to heal him. (The priests and producers of anointing oil were not happy that day.)

In fact, the entire story of Jesus is about a God who did not just want to stay "out there" but who moves into the neighborhood, a neighborhood where folks said, "Nothing good could come." It is this Jesus who was accused of being a glutton and drunkard and rabble-rouser for hanging out with all of society's rejects, and who died on the imperial cross of Rome reserved for bandits and failed messiahs. This is why the triumph over the cross was a triumph over everything ugly we do to ourselves and to others.

It is the final promise that love wins.

It is this Jesus who was born in a stank manger in the middle of a genocide. That is the God that we are just as likely to find in the streets as in the sanctuary, who can redeem revolutionaries and tax collectors, the oppressed and the oppressors... a God who is saving some of us from the ghettos of poverty, and some of us from the ghettos of wealth.

—Shane Claiborne

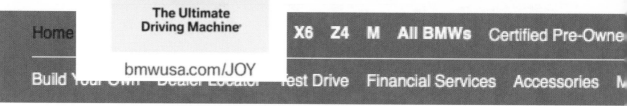

The Ultimate
Driving Machine®

Home | X6 Z4 M All BMWs Certified Pre-Owne

bmwusa.com/JOY

Build Your Own Dealer Locator Test Drive Financial Services Accessories M

"I think Jesus is setting us free from an oppressive way of life. I know plenty of people, both rich and poor, who are suffocating from the weight of the American dream, who find themselves heavily burdened by the lifeless toil and consumption put upon ourselves. This is the life we are being set free from. The new life is still not easy (it's a cross, for heaven's sake), but we carry it together, and it is good and leads us to rest, especially for the weariest traveler." —SHANE CLAIBORNE

AT BMW, WE DON'T JUST MAKE C

JOY IS AND. NOT OR.

BMW Members   Pieces of Heaven Art Aucti

JOY IS BMW EFFICIENT DYNAMICS

▸ More about BMW EfficientDynamics
information and save content.

VOGUE
ITALIA

JOY IS

JOY IS TIMELESS.

JOY IS INNOVATION.
95%

KE JOY.

JOY IS RECH...
THE BMW Concept ActiveE.

BMW EfficientDynamics
Less emissions. More driving pleasure.

JOY IS FUTUREPROOF.

See what's coming

Christianity offers the further insight that true fulfillment comes not from ego satisfaction, but through service to others. If I spend my life searching for happiness through drugs, comfort, and luxury it will elude me.

Jesus

captured succinctly the

paradoxical nature of life in

"Whoever finds his life will lose it,

and whoever loses his life for my

sake will find it." Such a statement

goes against the search for

"self-fulfillment" in advanced

psychology.

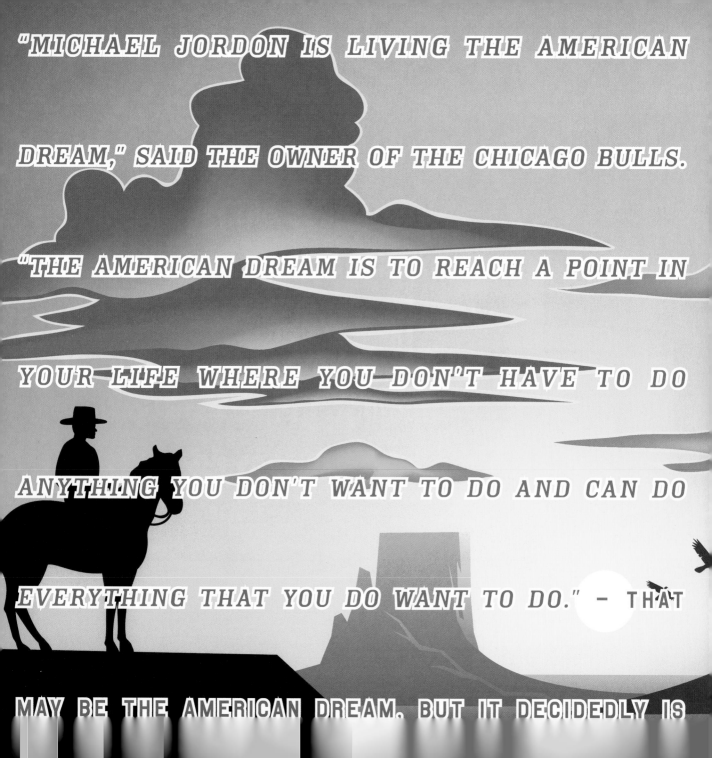

"MICHAEL JORDON IS LIVING THE AMERICAN DREAM," SAID THE OWNER OF THE CHICAGO BULLS. "THE AMERICAN DREAM IS TO REACH A POINT IN YOUR LIFE WHERE YOU DON'T HAVE TO DO ANYTHING YOU DON'T WANT TO DO AND CAN DO EVERYTHING THAT YOU DO WANT TO DO." – THAT MAY BE THE AMERICAN DREAM. BUT IT DECIDEDLY IS

NOT JESUS' DREAM AS REVEALED IN THE GOSPELS.

STRENGTH, GOOD LOOKS, CONNECTIONS, AND THE

COMPETITIVE INSTINCT MAY BRING A PERSON SUCCESS

IN A SOCIETY LIKE OURS, BUT THOSE VERY QUALITIES

MAY BLOCK ENTRANCE TO THE KINGDOM OF HEAVEN.

DEPENDENCE, SORROW, REPENTANCE, A LONGING TO

CHANGE—THESE ARE THE GATES TO GOD'S KINGDOM.

IN EXPERIMENTS, *WRITES ANNIE DILLARD,*

ENTOMOLOGISTS ENTICE

MALE BUTTERFLIES

WITH A

PAINTED CARDBOARD REPLICA

LARGER & MORE ENTICING THAN THE FEMALES

OF THEIR SPECIES.

EXCITED, THE MALE BUTTERFLY MOUNTS THE

PIECE OF CARDBOARD;

AGAIN AND AGAIN HE MOUNTS IT.

NEARBY,

THE REAL, LIVING FEMALE BUTTERFLY OPENS AND CLOSES HER WINGS IN VAIN.

POWER

FREEDOM

SUCCESS

PEACE

MONEY

WEALTH

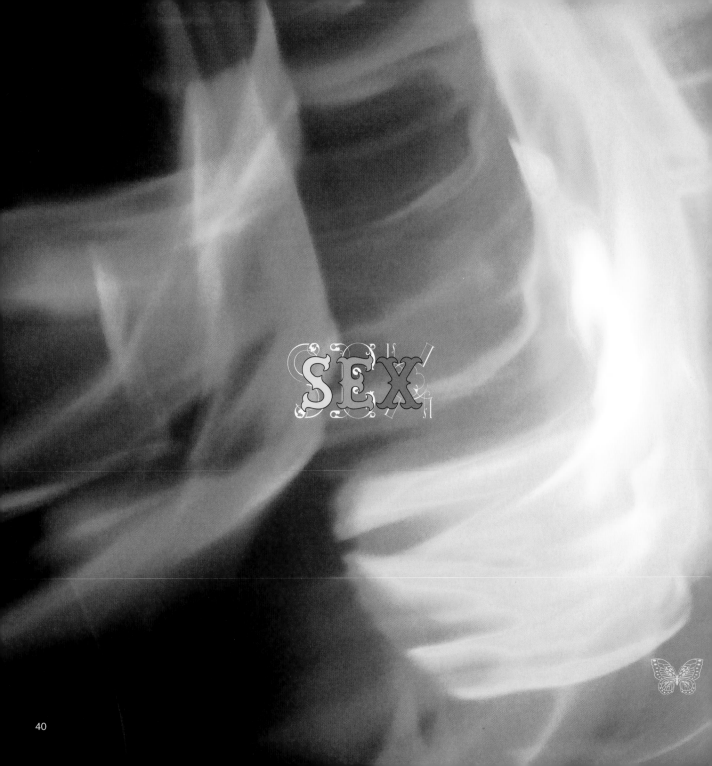

SEX

INTIMACY

PLEASURE

JOY

JESUS CAME, HE TOLD US, NOT TO DESTROY LIFE BUT THAT WE MAY HAVE IT MORE ABUNDANTLY, "LIFE TO THE FULL."

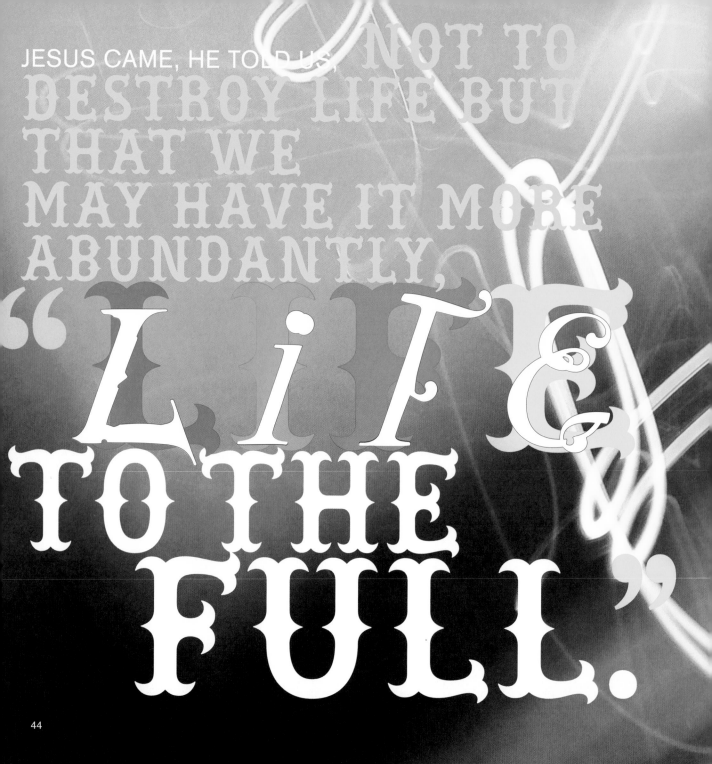

PARADOXICALLY, WE GET THIS ABUNDANT LIFE IN WAYS WE MAY NOT HAVE COUNTED ON. WE GET IT BY INVESTING IN OTHERS, BY TAKING COURAGEOUS STANDS FOR JUSTICE, BY MINISTERING TO THE WEAK AND NEEDY, BY PURSUING GOD AND NOT SELF.

The kingdom of heaven, Jesus said, is like a treasure of such value that any shrewd investor would "in his joy" sell all he has in order to buy it. It represents value far more real and permanent than anything the world has to offer, for this treasure will pay dividends both here on earth and also in the life to come. Jesus places the emphasis not on what we give up but on what we receive. Is it not in our own self-interest to pursue such a treasure?

✖ THE CLOSEST THING EVANGELICAL CHRISTIANS HAVE TO AN ICON—IN THE "SACRED PICTURE" SENSE OF THE WORD—IS THE CELEBRATED OIL PAINTING, *HEAD OF CHRIST*, BY WARNER SALLMAN. FIRST PUBLISHED IN 1940, IT'S NOW BEEN PRINTED MORE THAN 500,000,000 TIMES, MAKING IT THE MOST POPULAR RELIGIOUS IMAGE IN THE WORLD. PEOPLE CARRY IT IN THEIR WALLETS. IT HANGS IN EVERY SUNDAY SCHOOL ROOM FROM HERE TO JERUSALEM. AND NO MATTER HOW OLD YOU ARE, THIS PAINTING PROBABLY COMES TO MIND WHEN YOU THINK OF JESUS. (THIS AND, PERHAPS, A BLOODY JIM CAVIEZEL.) ✖ UNFORTUNATELY, THE IMAGE IS PROBABLY WRONG. I'M NOT A TRAINED ANTHROPOLOGIST, BUT SALLMAN'S JESUS—WITH HIS SHINY BRUSHED HAIR, NEATLY TRIMMED BEARD, LIMPID UPTURNED EYES, PLUCKED EYEBROWS, DELICATE NOSE AND FINE ANGLO CHEEKBONES—DOESN'T STRIKE ME AS VERY AUTHENTIC. JEWISH CARPENTERS JUST WEREN'T THAT PRETTY. ✖ **DON'T LET THE MANLY BEARD FOOL YOU:** SALLMAN TURNED JESUS INTO A WOMAN. ✖ *HEAD OF CHRIST* IS THE CAPSTONE IN A LONG HISTORY OF SENTIMENTAL FEMININE APPROACHES TO CHRIST, BEGINNING IN THE VICTORIAN ERA. BACK THEN, WOMEN DOMINATED THE CHURCH SCENE AND WERE BELIEVED TO BE MORALLY AND SPIRITUALLY SUPERIOR TO MEN. RELIGIOUS EDUCATION OCCURRED IN THE HOME, AND GUESS WHO RULED THE ROOST? THE PREVAILING VIEW OF JESUS TRICKLED DOWN INTO THE CULTURE FROM THESE PIOUS AND PURE MOMS. THE SERMON ON THE MOUNT WAS A FREQUENT TEXT, AND THEY EMPHASIZED THE STUFF ABOUT SACRIFICE AND SUBMISSION. THEIR JESUS BECAME A TENDER, LAMB-CARRYING GOOD SHEPHERD. ✖ WANT PROOF? CHECK OUT THE MAJOR PROTESTANT HYMNS COMPOSED DURING THIS TIME: "WHAT A FRIEND WE HAVE IN JESUS," BY JOSEPH SCRIVEN; "SOFTLY AND TENDERLY JESUS IS CALLING," BY WILLIAM L. THOMPSON; AND "GENTLE JESUS, MEEK AND MILD," BY CHARLES WESLEY. ✖ GOOD: THERE IS GREAT VALUE IN SERVANTHOOD AND HUMILITY, AND IT'S APPROPRIATE TO ASSOCIATE THOSE DIVINE QUALITIES WITH JESUS. ✖ BAD: PROPER HAIR CARE IS NOT A DIVINE QUALITY. AND GOOD LUCK GETTING THIS MEEK AND MILD PATSY TO WHIP MONEYCHANGERS OUT OF THE TEMPLE OR TO ENDURE THE BLOOD AND GUTS OF THE CROSS. ✖ —JASON BOYETT

The Old Testament underscores the vast gulf between God and humanity. God is supreme, omnipotent, transcendent, and any limited contact with him puts human beings at risk. The worship instructions in a book like Leviticus remind me of a manual on handling radioactive material.

—Bring only spotless lambs to the tabernacle.
—Do not touch the Ark.
—Always let smoke cover it;
—if you look at the ark, you'll die.
—Never enter the Most Holy Place, except for the high priest on the one permitted day of the year.
—On that day, Yom Kippur, fasten a rope around his ankle, and a bell, so that if he makes a mistake and dies inside, his corpse can be dragged out.

Jesus' disciples grew up in such an environment,
—never pronouncing God's name,
—complying with the intricate code of cleanliness, heeding the requirements of Mosaic law.

They took for granted, as did most other religions of the time, that worship must include sacrifice: something had to die. Their God had forbidden human sacrifice, and so on a festival day Jerusalem was filled with the bleats and cries of a quarter million animals destined for the temple altar. The noise and smell of sacrifice were sharp sensory reminders of the great gulf between God and themselves. I worked in the Old Testament for so long that, when one day I skipped over to the book of Acts, the contrast jolted me. Now God's followers, good Jews most of them, were meeting in private homes, singing hymns, and addressing God with the informal Abba. Where was the fear, and the solemn protocol required of anyone who dared approach mysterium tremendum? No one brought animals to sacrifice; death did not enter into worship except for the solemn moment when they broke bread and drank wine together, reflecting on the once-for-all sacrifice Jesus had made. In these ways, Jesus introduced profound changes in how we view God. Mainly, he brought God near. To Jews who knew a distant, ineffable God, Jesus brought the message that God cares for the grass of the field, feeds the sparrows, numbers the hairs on a person's head. To Jews who dared not pronounce the Name, Jesus brought the shocking intimacy of the Aramaic word Abba. It was a familiar term of family affection, onomatopoeic like "Dada," the first word many children spoke. Before Jesus, no one would have thought of applying such a word to Yahweh, the Sovereign Lord of the universe. After him, it became a standard term of address even in Greek-speaking congregations; imitating Jesus, they borrowed the foreign word to express their own intimacy with the Father. An event happened as Jesus hung on the cross that seemed to seal the new intimacy for the young church. Mark records that just as Jesus breathed his last, "The curtain of the temple was torn in two from top to bottom. " This massive curtain had served to wall off the Most Holy Place, where God's presence dwelled. As the author of Hebrews would later note, the tearing of this curtain showed beyond doubt exactly what was accomplished by Jesus' death. No more sacrifices would ever be required. No high priest need tremble to enter the sacred room. Those of us in modern times have lived under the new intimacy for so long that we take it for granted. We sing choruses to God and converse in casual prayers. To us, the notion of sacrifice seems primitive. Too easily we forget what it cost Jesus to win for us all—ordinary people, not just priests—immediate access to God's presence. We know God as Abba, the loving Father, only because of Jesus.

This is
the great reversal:
many of the first ending
up last,
and the last first.
—Jesus

Anyone who sacrifices home, family, fields—whatever—because of me will get it all back a hundred times over, not to mention the considerable bonus of eternal life.

"I TELL YOU THAT ANYONE WHO LOOKS AT A WOMAN LUSTFULLY HAS ALREADY COMMITTED ADULTERY WITH HER IN HIS HEART. IF YOUR RIGHT EYE CAUSES YOU TO SIN, GOUGE IT OUT AND THROW IT AWAY. IT IS BETTER FOR YOU TO LOSE ONE PART OF YOUR BODY THAN FOR YOUR WHOLE BODY TO BE THROWN INTO HELL."

—JESUS

"DO NOT RESIST AN EVIL PERSON. IF SOMEONE STRIKES YOU ON THE RIGHT CHEEK, TURN TO HIM THE OTHER ALSO. AND IF SOMEONE WANTS TO SUE YOU AND TAKE YOUR TUNIC, LET HIM HAVE YOUR CLOAK AS WELL."

—JESUS

Bernard L Madoff walks down Lexington Ave to his apartment December 17, 2008 in New York City. On June 30, 2009 the self-confessed author of the biggest financial swindle in history, was sentenced to the maximum 150 years behind bars for what his judge called an "extraordinarily evil" fraud that took "a staggering toll" on rich and poor alike.

53

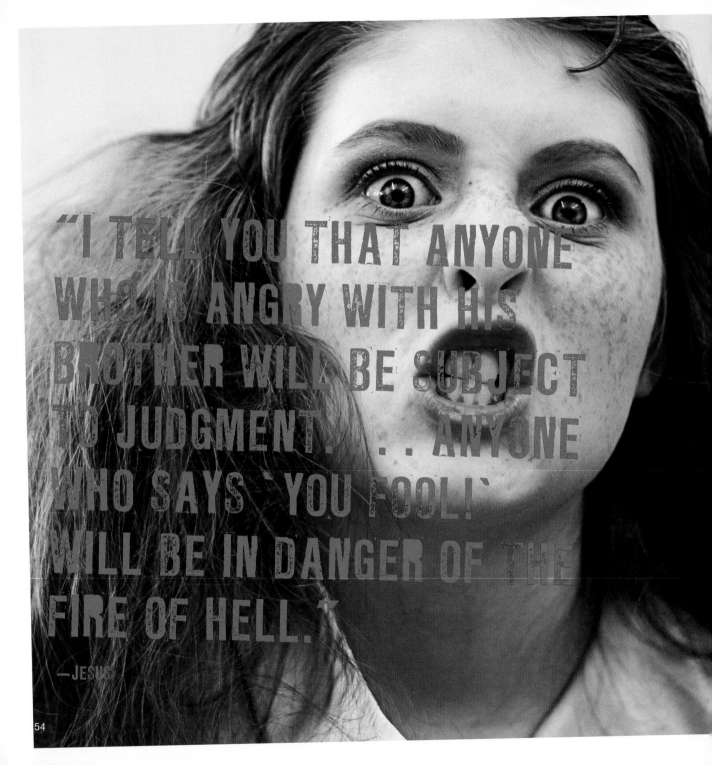

"I TELL YOU THAT ANYONE WHO IS ANGRY WITH HIS BROTHER WILL BE SUBJECT TO JUDGMENT. . . . ANYONE WHO SAYS `YOU FOOL!` WILL BE IN DANGER OF THE FIRE OF HELL."

—JESUS

54

"YOU'RE FAMILIAR WITH THE OLD WRITTEN LAW, 'LOVE YOUR FRIEND,' AND ITS UNWRITTEN COMPANION, 'HATE YOUR ENEMY.' I'M CHALLENGING THAT. I'M TELLING YOU TO LOVE YOUR ENEMIES."

—JESUS

Jesus never lowered God's Ideal. "Be perfect, therefore, as your heavenly Father is perfect," he said. "Love the Lord your God with all your heart and with all your soul and with all your mind." Not Mother Teresa, not anyone has completely fulfilled those commands.

WE WILL NEVER MEASURE UP.

Jesus forgave an adulteress, a thief on the cross, a disciple who had denied ever knowing him. He tapped that traitorous disciple, Peter, to found his church and for the next advance turned to a man named Saul, who had made his mark persecuting Christians. Grace is absolute, inflexible, all-encompassing. It extends even to the people who nailed Jesus to the cross: "Father, forgive them, for they do not know what they are doing" were among the last words Jesus spoke on earth.

There is only one way for any of us to resolve the tension between the high ideals of the gospel and the grim reality of ourselves: to accept that we will never measure up, but that we do not have to.

"There is now no condemnation for those who are in Christ Jesus"

BUT WE WILL NEVER HAVE TO

WHAT I LOVE ABOUT JESUS IS THAT HE ALWAYS HAS IMAGINATION. TALKING ABOUT THE FAMILIAR "TURN THE OTHER CHEEK" VERSES, AUTHOR AND PROFESSOR WALTER WINK POINTS OUT THAT JESUS IS NOT JUST SUGGESTING THAT WE MASOCHISTICALLY LET PEOPLE STEP ALL OVER US. INSTEAD, JESUS IS POINTING US TOWARD SOMETHING THAT IMAGINATIVELY DISARMS OTHERS. WHEN HIT ON THE CHEEK, TURN AND LOOK THE PERSON IN THE EYE. DO NOT COWER AND DO NOT PUNCH THEM BACK. MAKE SURE THEY LOOK INTO YOUR EYES AND SEE YOUR SACRED HUMANITY, AND IT WILL BECOME INCREASINGLY HARDER FOR THEM TO HURT YOU. WHEN SOMEONE TRIES TO SUE YOU FOR THE COAT ON YOUR BACK AND DRAGS YOU BEFORE THE COURT, GO AHEAD AND TAKE ALL OF YOUR CLOTHES OFF AND HAND THEM OVER, EXPOSING THE SICKNESS OF THEIR GREED. WHEN A SOLDIER ASKS YOU TO WALK A MILE WITH THEM AND CARRY THEIR PACK (AS WAS ROMAN LAW AND CUSTOM), WALK WITH THEM TWO MILES INSTEAD OF ONE, TALK WITH THEM AND WOO THEM INTO OUR MOVEMENT BY YOUR LOVE.

☐ Fight

☐ Flight

We a see a Jesus who abhors both passivity and violence, who carves out a third way that is neither submission or assault, neither fight nor flight. It is this third way, Wink writes, that teaches that 'evil can be opposed without being mirrored... oppressors can be resisted with out being emulated... enemies can be neutralized without being destroyed.' Then we can look into the eyes of a centurion and see not a beast but a child, and then walk with that child a couple of miles. Look into the eyes of tax collectors as they sue you in court. See their poverty and give them your coat. Look into the eyes of the ones who are hardest for you to like, and see the one you love."

—Shane Claiborne

"THE KINGDOM OF HEAVEN IS NEAR," HE PROCLAIMED IN HIS VERY FIRST MESSAGE. ✕ EACH TIME HE SPOKE IT, THAT WORD STIRRED MEMORIES TO LIFE: BRIGHT BANNERS, GLITTERING ARMIES, THE GOLD AND IVORY OF SOLOMON'S DAY, THE NATION OF ISRAEL RESTORED. WHAT WAS ABOUT TO HAPPEN, JESUS SAID, WOULD FAR SURPASS ANYTHING FROM THE PAST. ✕ ZEALOTS STOOD AT THE EDGE OF JESUS' AUDIENCE, ARMED AND WELL ORGANIZED GUERRILLAS SPOILING FOR A FIGHT AGAINST ROME, BUT THE SIGNAL FOR REVOLT NEVER CAME. ✕ IN TIME, JESUS' PATTERN OF BEHAVIOR DISAPPOINTED ALL WHO SOUGHT A LEADER IN THE TRADITIONAL MOLD. THE ONE TIME A CROWD TRIED TO CROWN HIM KING BY FORCE, HE MYSTERIOUSLY WITHDREW. AND WHEN PETER FINALLY DID WIELD A SWORD ON HIS BEHALF, JESUS HEALED THE VICTIM'S WOUNDS. ✕ TO THE CROWDS' DISMAY, IT BECAME CLEAR THAT JESUS WAS TALKING ABOUT A STRANGELY DIFFERENT KIND OF KINGDOM. THE JEWS WANTED WHAT PEOPLE HAVE ALWAYS WANTED FROM A VISIBLE KINGDOM: A CHICKEN IN EVERY POT, FULL EMPLOYMENT, A STRONG ARMY TO DETER INVADERS. JESUS ANNOUNCED A KINGDOM THAT MEANT DENYING YOURSELF, TAKING UP A CROSS, RENOUNCING WEALTH, EVEN LOVING YOUR ENEMIES. ✕ AS HE ELABORATED, THE CROWD'S EXPECTATIONS CRUMBLED.

He was frequently sad and sometimes depressed.

Because
God loves the poor,
the suffering,
the persecuted, so
should we. Because God
sees no undesirables,
neither should we.

Normally in this world we look up to the rich, the beautiful, the successful. Jesus, however, introduced a world of new logic.

Jesus did not mechanically follow a list of "Things I Gotta Do Today," and I doubt he would have appreciated our modern emphasis on punctuality and precise scheduling. He attended wedding feasts that lasted for days. He let himself get distracted by any "nobody" he came across, whether a hemorrhaging woman who shyly touched his robe or a blind beggar who made a nuisance of himself. Two of his most impressive miracles (the raising of Lazarus and of Jairus's daughter) took place because he arrived too late to heal the sick person.

Jesus was "the man for others." He kept himself free – free for the other person. He would >

Tony Blair and U2 singer Bono greeting other participants at a discussion of Africa.

AMSTERDAM Two ex-prostitutes, both former heavy drug users, hug a sex worker in Amsterdam's Red Light district. Through religious faith, they both kicked off their addiction and spend much of their time healing others.

accept almost anybody's invitation to dinner, and as a result >

USA.
A group of bikers pray on the beach. Although they have adopted their tattoos and wear identical paraphernalia, they are no Hells Angels. They are Bikers for Christ, ministering to fellow bikers some of whom are outlaws.

no public figure had a more diverse list of friends, ranging from rich people, >

roman centurions,
and religious leaders to
tax collectors, >

KERKORISOGOL, Turkana, Kenya, Oct. 24, 2008. Ekomol and other Turkana women divide up corn received in World Vision food distribution. Shadrack Mutiso works with food monitor, Celine Ekitela Achuku, 23, to ensure the food is distributed evenly with a peaceful dignity.

CINCINNATI.
2002 Billy Graham. An estimated 201,600 people turned out at Paul Brown Stadium over the four day mission to bring healing and to encourage racial harmony in the area.

prostitutes, and leprosy victims. People liked being with Jesus; >

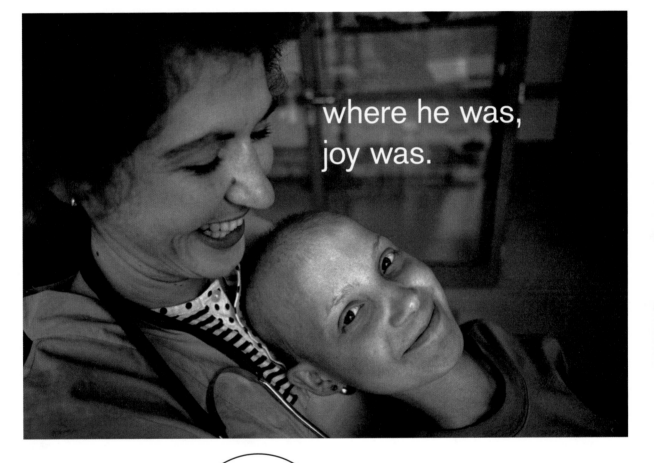

where he was,
joy was.

BELARUS.
Minsk.
Childrens Cancer
Hospital. A young orphan
who is undergoing
chemotherapy has adopted
every doctor as her
"new mother."

I first
got acquainted
with Jesus when I was a child,
singing "Jesus Loves Me" in Sunday
school, addressing bedtime prayers to "Dear
Lord Jesus," watching Bible Club teachers
move cutout figures across a flannelgraph board.
I associated Jesus with Kool-Aid and sugar cookies
and gold stars for good attendance. —— Recently, I
read a book that the elderly Charles Dickens had written
to sum up the life of Jesus for his children. In it, the
portrait emerges of a sweet Victorian nanny who pats
the heads of boys and girls. With a start I recalled
the Sunday School image of Jesus I grew up
with: someone kind and reassuring, with
no sharp edges at all. As a child I felt
comforted by such a
person.

Jesus grew and became strong; stayed in Jerusalem. listening to them asking questions. answered went back with them grew up, gaining favor was baptized. praying, began his work returned full of the Holy Spirit, was tempted by the Devil for forty days. ate nothing was hungry The Devil said to him, Jesus answered, the Devil took him up and showed him all the kingdoms of the world. Jesus answered, the Devil set him on the highest point of the Temple, Jesus answered returned to Galilee, He taught went to Nazareth, stood up to read unrolled the scroll found the place rolled up the scroll, sat down. began speaking to them: They rose up, dragged Jesus to the top of the hill to throw him over the cliff. But he walked through the middle of the crowd went his way. went to Capernaum, taught his words had authority. commanded the spirit: left stood at her bedside, gave a command placed his hands on every one healed them all. would not let them speak, went off to a lonely place. preached was standing saw two boats got into one asked him to push off sat taught finished speaking, said to Simon, "Don't be afraid; reached out touched a man who was covered with leprosy. ordered would go away to lonely places, prayed. teaching, saw faith said "Your sins are forgiven knew their thoughts said to the paralyzed man, get up, went out saw said "Follow me." eat and drink with outcasts told them this parable was walking through some wheat fields went taught. knew looked around said to the man, "Stretch out your hand." went up a hill spent the whole night praying called chose twelve stood power was going out from him and healing them all. looked told them finished saying all these things went with them. was surprised turned around went to a town named Nain; arrived saw a widow, his heart was filled with pity said "Don't cry." walked over touched the coffin, gave him back to his mother. healed many from their sicknesses, diseases, and evil spirits, and gave sight to many blind people. answered began to speak went to his house sat down to eat. spoke up began; turned to the woman said to the woman, "Your sins are forgiven." made a trip through towns preaching the Good News about the Kingdom of God. People kept coming to Jesus Jesus' mother and brothers came to him, got into a boat went to sleep. got up gave a command to the wind and to the stormy water; said "Where is your faith?" sailed stepped ashore, was met by a man who had demons in him. The demons begged Jesus asked Jesus to go away, got into the boat and left. sent him away, returned to the other side went along, people were crowding him She touched the edge of his cloak, asked, "Who touched me?" said to her, "My daughter, heard it said to Jairus, "Don't be afraid; arrived at the house would not let anyone go in took her by the hand called out, "Get up, child!" commanded them not to tell anyone called gave them power and authority to drive out all demons and to cure diseases. sent them out to preach and to heal the sick. took them with him welcomed them, spoke to them took the five loaves and two fish, looked up to heaven, thanked God broke them, gave them was praying alone, gave them strict orders not to tell this went up a hill to pray. his face changed its appearance and his clothes became dazzling white. a large crowd met Jesus. said to the man, "Bring your son here." gave a command to the evil spirit, healed the boy, gave him back to his father. knew what they were thinking, took a child, stood him by his side, made up his mind set out on his way sent messengers ahead turned and rebuked them; went on

chose another seventy-two men sent them out, was about to go. answered was filled with joy a certain teacher tried to trap Jesus.

answered: came to a certain village where Martha welcomed him in her home. was praying said "This is what you should pray:

was driving out a demon that could not talk; crowds were amazed, Others wanted to trap him, people crowded around Jesus

finished speaking, a Pharisee invited him to eat with him; so he went in and sat down left that place thousands of people crowded

A man in the crowd said to him, answered him, went on to say to them all: told them this parable: Jesus said also to the people:

told them this parable: teaching in a synagogue. saw woman there who had an evil spirit called out to her, "Woman, you are free

placed his hands on her His answer made all his enemies ashamed all the people rejoiced over every wonderful thing that he did.

went through towns and villages, teaching Someone asked him, went to eat a meal spoke up took the man, healed him

sent him away. noticed how some of the guests were choosing the best places, told this parable said to his host:

Great crowds of people were going along with Jesus. turned and said outcasts came to listen to Jesus. told them this parable:

they made fun of Jesus made his way to Jerusalem was met by ten lepers. said to them, He threw himself to the ground at Jesus' feet,

spoke up: said to him, "Get up and go; your faith has made you well." told this parable, Some people brought their babies to Jesus

called the children asked him. saw that he was sad took the twelve disciples aside Jesus stopped and ordered that the blind man

be brought to him. asked him, "What do you want me to do for you?" went on into Jericho looked up and said to Zacchaeus,

told a parable went on to Jerusalem sent two disciples rode on, came closer to the city when he saw it he wept over it,

went into the Temple began to drive out the merchants, taught in the Temple every day. the chief priests tried to arrest Jesus

saw through their trick the whole crowd listened to him, looked around and saw rich men saw a very poor widow

told them this parable: spent those days teaching in the Temple, spend the night on the Mount of Olives. sent Peter and John

took his place at the table took the cup, gave thanks to God, took the bread, gave thanks to God, broke it, and gave it

gave them the cup, went to the Mount of Olives; went off from them, knelt down prayed. his sweat was like drops of blood,

found them asleep, Judas, came up to Jesus to kiss him. He touched the man's ear and healed him. They arrested Jesus

The men guarding Jesus made fun of him and beat him. The chief priests and the teachers made strong accusations against Jesus.

Herod and his soldiers made fun of Jesus treated him with contempt. The whole crowd cried out, "Kill him! "To the cross with him!

They took Jesus away. they nailed Jesus to the cross Jesus said, "Forgive them, Father! the Jewish leaders made fun of him:

Jesus said 'today you will be in Paradise with me." Jesus cried out in a loud voice, "Father! In your hands I place my spirit!"

He said this and died. he has risen. Jesus himself drew near walked along with them; sat at table with them, took the bread,

said the blessing; broke the bread gave it disappeared from sight. suddenly stood among them showed them his hands and his feet.

ate led them out of the city raised his hands and blessed them. departed from them, was taken up into heaven.

Self-
sacrifice is
the way, my way, to
finding yourself, your
true self. What kind of deal
is it to get everything you
want but lose yourself?
What could you ever
trade your soul for?
—Jesus

Anyone
who intends to
come with me has to
let me lead. You're not
in the driver's seat; I am.
Don't run from suffering;
embrace it. Follow me
and I'll show you how.
Self-help is no help
at all.

SUS
WAS
A

JESUS WAS A HUNCHBACK.

One tradition dating back to the second century suggested

In the Middle Ages, Christians widely believed that

Most Christians today would find such notions repulsive and perhaps heretical.

Was he not a perfect specimen of humanity? Yet in all the Bible I can find

only one physical description of sorts, a prophecy written hundreds of years

before Christ's birth. Here is Isaiah's portrayal, in the midst of a passage that

the New Testament applies to the life of Jesus:

> Just as there were many who were appalled at him—his appearance was so disfigured beyond that of any man and his form marred beyond human likeness.
> . . . He had no beauty or majesty to attract us to him, nothing in his appearance that we should desire him. He was despised and rejected by men, a man of sorrows, and familiar with suffering. Like one from whom men hide their faces he was despised, and we esteemed him not.

BECAUSE OF THE GOSPELS' SILENCE, we cannot answer with certainty the basic question of what Jesus looked like. That is a good thing, I believe. Our glamorized representations of Jesus say more about us than about him. He had no supernatural glow about him: John the Baptist admitted he never would have recognized Jesus apart from special revelation. According to Isaiah, we cannot point to his beauty or majesty or anything else in his appearance to explain his attraction. The key lies elsewhere.

BELARUS. Children's Cancer Hospital, Minsk.
Mother and daughter.

Hebrews tells us, Jesus "offered up...loud cries and tears to the one who could save him from death." But of course he was not saved from death. Is it too much to say that Jesus himself asked the question that haunts me, that haunts most of us at one time or another: **Does God care?** What else can be the meaning of his quotation from that dark psalm, "My God, my God, why have you forsaken me?"

I find it strangely comforting that when Jesus faced pain he responded much as I do. He did not pray in the garden, "Oh, Lord, I am so grateful that you have chosen me to suffer on your behalf. I rejoice in the privilege!" No, he experienced sorrow, fear, abandonment, and something approaching even desperation. Still, he endured because he knew that at the center of the universe lived his Father, a God of love he could trust regardless of how things appeared at the time.

A man with leprosy came to Jesus and begged him on his
knees, "If you are willing, you can make me clean."

Filled with compassion,

Jesus reached out his hand and touched the man.

NETHERLANDS
Evangelists pray
for a crack addict in
Amsterdam's Red-Light
district. The evangelists
are former addicts
themselves.

Jesus raised his friend Lazarus from the dead, and a few years later, Lazarus died
again. Jesus healed the sick, but they eventually caught some other disease. He fed
the thousands, and the next day they were hungry again. But we remember his love.
It wasn't that Jesus healed a leper but that he touched a leper, because no one
touched lepers. —Shane Claiborne

Those of us in the twentieth century, an era that has few literal "kings," conceive of kingdoms in terms of power and polarization. We are the children of revolution. Two centuries ago in the U. S. and France the oppressed rose up and overturned the reigning powers. Later, in places like Russia and China, Marxists led revolts with an ideology that became a kind of religion: they began, in fact, to view all history as an outgrowth of class struggle, or dialectical materialism. "Workers, unite! Throw off your chains!" cried Marx, and so they did for much of our bloody century. For a period of time I tried to read the Gospels through the eyes of liberation theology. Ultimately I had to conclude that, whatever else it is, the kingdom of God is decidedly not a call to violent revolution. First century Jews were doubtless looking for such an upheaval. Battle lines were clear: oppressed Jews versus the bad-guy Romans—pagans who collected taxes, trafficked in slaves, regulated religion, and quashed dissent. Under these conditions the Zealots issued a call much like Marx's: "Jews, unite! Throw off your chains!" But Jesus' message of the kingdom had little in common with the politics of polarization. As I read the Gospels, Jesus seems to speak a two-pronged message. To the oppressors, he had words of warning and judgment. He treated the powers of government with an attitude of mild contempt, dismissing Herod as "that fox" (a Jewish expression for a worthless or insignificant person) and agreeing to pay a temple tax "so that we may not offend them." He placed little store in politics; it was government, after all, that tried to exterminate him. To the oppressed, his primary audience, Jesus offered a message of comfort and consolation. He called the poor and the persecuted "blessed." Never did he incite the oppressed to rise up and throw off their chains. In words that must have galled the Zealots, he commanded, "Love your enemies."

HE INVOKED A DIFFERENT KIND OF POWER:

LOVE, NOT COERCION. People who looked to Jesus as their political savior were constantly befuddled by his choice of companions. He became known as a friend of tax collectors, a group clearly identified with the foreign exploiters, not the exploited. Though he denounced the religious system of his day, he treated a leader like Nicodemus with respect, and though he spoke against the dangers of money and of violence, he showed love and compassion toward a rich young ruler and a Roman centurion. In short, Jesus honored the dignity of people, whether he agreed with them or not. He would not found his kingdom on the basis of race or class or other such divisions. Anyone, even a half-breed with five husbands or a thief dying on a cross, was welcome to join his kingdom. The person was more important than any category or label. I feel convicted by this quality of Jesus every time I get involved in a cause I strongly believe in. How easy it is to join the politics of polarization, to find myself shouting across the picket lines at the "enemy" on the other side. How hard it is to remember that the kingdom of God calls me to love the woman who has just emerged from the abortion clinic (and, yes, even her doctor), the promiscuous person who is dying of AIDS, the wealthy landowner who is exploiting God's creation. If I cannot show love to such people, then I must question whether I have truly understood Jesus' gospel. A political movement by nature draws lines, makes distinctions, pronounces judgment; in contrast, Jesus' love cuts across lines, transcends distinctions, and dispenses grace. Regardless of the merits of a given issue—whether a pro-life lobby out of the Right or a peace-and-justice lobby out of the Left— political movements risk pulling onto themselves the mantle of power that smothers love. From Jesus I learn that, whatever activism I get involved in, it must not drive out love and humility, or otherwise I betray the kingdom of heaven.

Despite the shame and sadness of it all, somehow what took place on a hill called Calvary became arguably the most important fact of Jesus' life—for the writers of the Gospels and Epistles, for the church, and, as far as we can speculate on such matters, for God as well. It took time for the church to come to terms with the ignominy of the cross. Church fathers forbade its depiction in art until the reign of the Roman emperor Constantine, who had seen a vision of the cross and who also banned it as a method of execution. Thus not until the fourth century did the cross become a symbol of the faith. (As C. S. Lewis points out, the crucifixion did not become common in art until all who had seen a real one died off.) Now, though, the symbol is everywhere: artists beat gold into the shape of the Roman execution device, baseball players cross themselves before batting, and candy confectioners even make chocolate crosses for the faithful to eat during Holy Week. Strange as it may seem, Christianity has become a religion of the cross—the gallows, the electric chair, the gas chamber, in modern terms. /// By the time he was nailed to wooden crossbeams, everyone had lost hope and fallen away. As for the Twelve, no matter how often or how plainly Jesus warned them of his impending death, it never sank in.

NO ONE COULD IMAGINE A MESSIAH DYING. What did Jesus mean by the kingdom of God? The word kingdom meant one thing to Jesus and quite another to the crowd. Jesus was rejected, in large part, because he did not measure up to a national image of what a Messiah was supposed to look like. A question has long puzzled me. In view of their expectations, why did Jesus keep arousing his followers' hopes with the word kingdom? He insisted on associating himself with a term that everyone seemed to misunderstand. Jesus never offered a clear definition of the kingdom; instead he imparted his vision of it indirectly through a series of stories.

His choice of images is telling: everyday sketches of farming, fishing, women baking bread, merchants buying pearls. The kingdom of heaven is like a farmer going out to sow his seed. As every farmer knows, not all the seed you plant ends up yielding crops. Some falls among rocks, some gets eaten by birds and field mice, some gets crowded out by weeds. All this seems natural to a farmer, but heretical to a traditional kingdom-builder. Are not kings judged by their power, their ability to impose their will on a populace, their strength in repelling enemies? Jesus was indicating that the kingdom of God comes with a resistible power. It is humble and unobtrusive and coexistent with evil—a message that surely did not please patriotic Jews intent on revolt. Consider the mustard seed, a seed so tiny it can fall to the ground and lie unnoticed by human beings and birds alike. Given time, though, the seed may sprout into a bush that overtakes every other plant in the garden, a bush so large and verdant that birds come and nest in its branches. God's kingdom works like that. It begins so small that people scorn it and give it no chance for success. Against all odds, God's kingdom will grow and spread throughout the world, bringing shade to the sick, the poor, the imprisoned, the unloved. The kingdom of heaven is like a businessman who specializes in rare gems. One day he finds a pearl gorgeous enough to make princesses drool with envy. Recognizing its value, he liquidates his entire business in order to buy it. Although the purchase costs everything he owns, not for a moment does he regret it. He makes the trade with joy, as the crowning achievement of his life: the treasure will outlive him, enduring long after the family name has disappeared. God's kingdom works like that. The sacrifice—deny yourself, take up your cross—turns out to be a shrewd investment, its outcome not remorse but joy beyond all telling. These are the stories Jesus told.

Jesus' healings are not supernatural miracles in a natural world. They are the only truly 'natural' things in a world that is unnatural, demonized and wounded.

LUCKY

UNLUCKY.

THOUGH I HAVE TRIED AT TIMES TO DISMISS IT AS
RHETORICAL EXCESS, THE MORE I STUDY JESUS, THE
MORE I REALIZE THAT THE STATEMENTS CONTAINED IN
HIS SERMON ON THE MOUNT LIE AT THE HEART OF HIS
MESSAGE. IF I FAIL TO UNDERSTAND THIS TEACHING, I
FAIL TO UNDERSTAND HIM. JESUS DELIVERED THE FAMOUS
SERMON AT A TIME WHEN HIS POPULARITY WAS SOARING.
CROWDS PURSUED HIM WHEREVER HE WENT, OBSESSED WITH
ONE QUESTION: HAS THE MESSIAH COME AT LAST? ON
THIS UNUSUAL OCCASION JESUS SKIPPED THE PARABLES
AND GRANTED HIS AUDIENCE A FULL-BLOWN "PHILOSOPHY
OF LIFE" SOMEWHAT LIKE A CANDIDATE UNVEILING A
NEW POLITICAL PLATFORM. WHAT A PLATFORM. JESUS
KNEW HOW LIFE WORKS, IN THE KINGDOM OF HEAVEN
AS WELL AS THE KINGDOM OF THIS WORLD.

ARE THE

The Beatitudes (blessings):

"BLESSED ARE THE POOR IN SPIRIT,
   FOR THEIRS IS THE KINGDOM OF HEAVEN.
BLESSED ARE THOSE WHO MOURN,
   FOR THEY WILL BE COMFORTED.
BLESSED ARE THE MEEK,
   FOR THEY WILL INHERIT THE EARTH.
BLESSED ARE THOSE WHO HUNGER AND THIRST FOR RIGHTEOUSNESS,
   FOR THEY WILL BE FILLED.
BLESSED ARE THE MERCIFUL,
   FOR THEY WILL BE SHOWN MERCY.
BLESSED ARE THE PURE IN HEART,
   FOR THEY WILL SEE GOD.
BLESSED ARE THE PEACEMAKERS,
   FOR THEY WILL BE CALLED SONS OF GOD.
BLESSED ARE THOSE WHO ARE PERSECUTED BECAUSE OF RIGHTEOUSNESS,
   FOR THEIRS IS THE KINGDOM OF HEAVEN."

Any Greek scholar will tell you the word "blessed" is far too sedate to carry the percussive force Jesus intended. The Greek word conveys something like a short cry of joy,

"Oh, you lucky person!"

LUCKY ARE

HAITI 2010 A survivor in Carrefour.
Earthquake aftermath.

THE UNLUCKY?

HAITI. Port-Au-Prince. 2010. Carrel RAPHAEL, a Haitian 'Tap-Tap' driver who lost his wife and two of his children in the earthquake just after returning to his neighborhood.

UNLUCKY?

Bill Gates Huge Residence finally reaches completion after 4 years of work. The 5,000-square-meter palace the richest man on Earth has had built on 2 hectares of land on the shore of Lake Washington in Medina, June 2, 1998.

LUCKY?

USA. New York. Homeless man
passed out on a train.

UNLUCKY?

Pittsburgh Steelers Ben Roethlisberger (7) in action vs Tennessee Titans.

LUCKY?

AMAICA. Kingston. Bethlehem Center
(Children's Center), 10:30 - 12:00 noon.

UNITED STATES : Matthew Fergueson, president and chief executive officer of CareerBuilder.com, speaks at a session on talent management during the National Summit in Detroit, Michigan, U.S., on Wednesday June 17, 2009.

UNLUCKY?

UNITED STATES Job seekers line up outside of the Metropolitan Pavilion for a Careerbuilder.com career fair in New York, U.S., on Thursday, April 2, 2009. The number of Americans seeking jobless benefits climbed to the highest level in 26 years.

LUCKY?

UNLUCKY?

INDIA. West Bengal, Calcutta. A woman with burn scars begs at the Oberoi Hotel.

LUCKY?

****

LUCKY are the strong.
******

LUCKY ARE THE TRIUMPHANT.
****

****

LUCKY are the armies
wealthy enough to possess
smart bombs and patriot
missiles.
****

LUCKY are the liberators,
the CONQUERING soldiers.
***

??????

IN A GROUND CAMPAIGN that lasted a scant one hundred hours, allied forces had achieved a stunning victory over Iraq in the Gulf War. Like most Americans, I could hardly believe the longfeared war had ended so quickly, with so few American casualties. CNN announced an interruption in scheduled programming: they would shift to live coverage of the morning-after press conference by the commander of allied forces. For a time I tried to continue preparing for my class. I watched five minutes of Pasolini's version of Jesus delivering the Beatitudes, then several minutes of General Schwarzkopf 's version of allied troops bearing down on Kuwait City. Soon I abandoned the VCR altogether—Stormin' Norman proved entirely too engaging. He told of the "end run" around Iraq's elite Republican Guard, of a decoy invasion by sea, of the allied capability of marching all the way to Baghdad unopposed. A general confident in his mission and immensely proud of the soldiers who had carried it out, Schwarzkopf gave a bravura performance. I remember thinking, That's exactly the person you want to lead a war. ***************************The briefing ended, CNN switched to commercials, and I returned to the VCR tapes. Max von Sydow, a blond, pasty Jesus, was giving an improbable rendition of the Sermon on the Mount in *The Greatest Story Ever Told.*

"BLESSED *(lucky)* ARE . . . THE . . . POOR . . . IN SPIRIT," *he intoned in a slow, thick Scandinavian accent,* "FOR . . . THEIRS . . . IS . . THE . . KINGDOM . . . OF . . . HEAVEN." **************** I had to adjust to the languid pace of the movie compared to General Schwarzkopf's briefing, and it took a few seconds for the irony to sink in: I had just been watching the Beatitudes in reverse! ***************************************

The bizarre juxtaposition of two speeches gave me a feeling for the shock waves the Sermon on the Mount must have caused among its original audience, Jews in first-century Palestine. Instead of General Schwarzkopf, they had Jesus, and to a downtrodden people yearning for emancipation from Roman rule, Jesus gave startling and unwelcome advice. If an enemy soldier slaps you, turn the other cheek. Rejoice in persecution. Be grateful for your poverty.

???

LUCKY are those who mourn?

Because I have written books with titles like *Where Is God When It Hurts?* and *Disappointment with God*, I have spent time among mourners. They intimidated me at first. I had few answers for the questions they were asking, and I felt awkward in the presence of their grief. I remember especially one year when, at the invitation of a neighbor, I joined a therapy group at a nearby hospital. This group, called Make Today Count, consisted of people who were dying, and I accompanied my neighbor to their meetings for a year.

Certainly I cannot say that I "enjoyed" the gatherings; that would be the wrong word. Yet the meetings became for me one of the most meaningful events of each month. In contrast to a party, where participants try to impress each other with signs of status and power, in this group no one was trying to impress. Clothes, fashions, apartment furnishings, job titles, new cars—what do these things mean to people who are preparing to die?

Later, when I wrote about what I had learned from grieving and suffering people, I began hearing from strangers. I have three folders, each one several inches thick, filled with these letters. They are among my most precious possessions. One letter, twenty-six pages long, was written on blue-lined note paper by a mother sitting in a lounge outside a room where surgeons were operating on her four-year-old daughter's brain tumor. Another came from a quadriplegic who "wrote" by making puffs of air into a tube, which a computer translated into letters on a printer.

Many of the people who have written me have no happy endings to their stories. Some still feel abandoned by God. Few have found answers to the "Why?" questions. But I have seen enough grief that I have gained faith in Jesus' promise that those who mourn will be comforted.

In the Beatitudes, Jesus honored people who may not enjoy many privileges in this life. To the poor, the mourners, the meek, the hungry, the persecuted, the poor in heart, he offered assurance that their service would not go unrecognized. They would receive ample reward. "IF WE CONSIDER THE UNBLUSHING PROMISES OF REWARD AND THE STAGGERING NATURE OF THE REWARDS PROMISED IN THE GOSPELS, IT WOULD SEEM THAT OUR LORD FINDS OUR DESIRES, NOT TOO STRONG, BUT TOO WEAK. WE ARE HALF-HEARTED CREATURES, FOOLING ABOUT WITH SEX AND DRINK AND AMBITION WHEN INFI

"INFINITE JOY IS OFFERED US, LIKE AN IGNORANT CHILD WHO WANTS TO GO ON MAKING MUD PIES IN A SLUM BECAUSE HE CANNOT IMAGINE WHAT IS MEANT BY THE OFFER OF A HOLIDAY AT THE SEA."

C.S. LEWIS

LUCKY ARE THE DESPER-ATE?

With
nowhere else
to turn,
the desperate
just may turn
to Jesus,
the only one
who can
offer the
deliverance
they
long for.

109

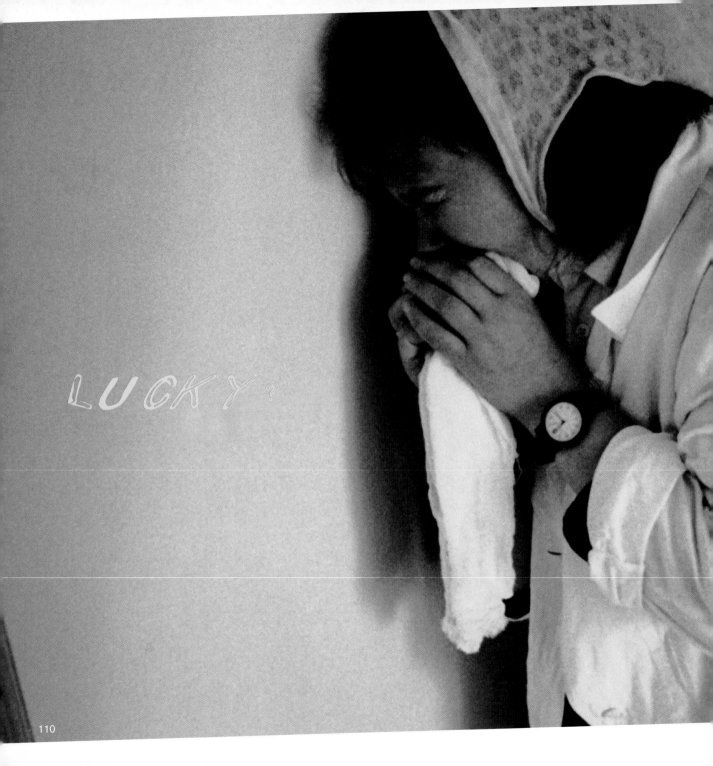

LUCKY?

BELARUS.
Gonel. Intensive therapy
Hematology Unit at the Gonel
regional Clinical hospital. Aleysa
Beoia, 17 years old, has leukemia that
was first diagnosed when she was 11
years old. Although Aleysa was treated in
Russia, Ireland, USA and Belarus during
that six years, none of the treatments
worked. Her mother, Lida, cries in
the hallway after Aleysa dies
in the hospital.

President Bill Clinton, alarmed about his low standing among evangelical Christians, summoned twelve of us to a private breakfast in order to hear our concerns. Each of us would have five minutes to say whatever we wanted the president and vice president to hear. The question, "What would Jesus say in such a setting?" crossed my mind, and I realized with a start that the only time Jesus met with powerful political leaders, his hands were tied and his back was clotted with blood. Church and state have had an uneasy relationship ever since. I turned to the Beatitudes and found myself startled anew. What if I translated their message into contemporary terms?

Mr. President, First I want to advise you to stop worrying so much about the economy and jobs. A lower Gross National Product is actually good for the country. Don't you understand that the poor are the fortunate ones? The more poor we have in the U.S., the more blessed we are. Theirs is the kingdom of heaven. And don't devote so much time to health care. You see, Mr. President, those who mourn are blessed too, for they'll be comforted. I know you've heard from the Religious Right about the increasing secularization of our country. Prayer is no longer allowed in schools, and protesters against abortion are subject to arrest. Relax, sir. Government oppression gives Christians an opportunity to be persecuted, and therefore blessed. Thank you for the expanded opportunities.

GAMES

STYLE

RED CARPET

PHOTOS

NEWS

HOME

CELEBRITY CENTRAL

TOP 25 CELEBS ▶

ENDORSEMENT IMPLIED

UN

people

114

AGAIN!

I WANT A
DIVORCE
SUICIDE

Cate Blanchett

Catherine Zeta-Jones

Chace Crawford

Channing Tatum

Charlize Theron

Cheryl Burke

Chris Brown

Chris Pine

Christina Applegate

Christina Aguilera

Claire Danes

Clay Aiken

Colin Farrell

Corbin Bleu

Courteney Cox Arquette

Leonardo DiCaprio

Hayden Panettiere

Heath Ledger

commits suicide

Ali Larter

Alicia Keys

Amanda Bynes

America Ferrera

Madonna

UNLUCKY ARE THE LUCKY?

My career as a journalist has afforded me opportunities to
interview "stars," including NFL football greats, movie actors,
music performers, bestselling authors, politicians, and TV
personalities. These are the people who dominate the media.
We fawn over them, poring over the minutiae of their lives:
the clothes they wear, the food they eat, the aerobic routines
they follow, the people they love, the toothpaste they use. Yet
I must tell you that, in my limited experience, I have found that
our "idols" are as miserable a group of people as I have ever
met. Most have troubled or broken marriages. Nearly all are
incurably dependent on psychotherapy. In a heavy irony, these
larger-than-life heroes seem tormented by self-doubt.

I HAVE SPENT TIME WITH PEOPLE I CALL "SERVANTS." DOCTORS AND NURSES WHO WORK AMONG THE ULTIMATE OUTCASTS. LEPROSY PATIENTS IN RURAL INDIA, A PRINCETON GRADUATE WHO RUNS A HOTEL FOR THE HOMELESS IN CHICAGO, HEALTH WORKERS WHO HAVE LEFT HIGH-PAYING JOBS TO SERVE IN A BACKWATER TOWN OF MISSISSIPPI, RELIEF WORKERS IN SOMALIA, SUDAN, ETHIOPIA, BANGLADESH, AND OTHER REPOSITORIES OF HUMAN SUFFERING. THE PH.D.S I MET IN ARIZONA, WHO ARE NOW SCATTERED THROUGHOUT JUNGLES OF SOUTH AMERICA TRANSLATING THE BIBLE INTO OBSCURE LANGUAGES. I WAS PREPARED TO HONOR AND ADMIRE THESE SERVANTS, TO HOLD THEM UP AS INSPIRING EXAMPLES. I WAS NOT PREPARED TO ENVY THEM. YET AS I NOW REFLECT ON THE TWO GROUPS SIDE BY SIDE, STARS AND SERVANTS, THE SERVANTS CLEARLY EMERGE AS THE FAVORED ONES, THE GRACED ONES. WITHOUT QUESTION, I WOULD RATHER SPEND TIME AMONG THE SERVANTS THAN AMONG THE STARS: THEY POSSESS QUALITIES OF DEPTH AND RICHNESS AND EVEN JOY THAT I HAVE NOT FOUND ELSEWHERE. SERVANTS WORK FOR LOW PAY, LONG HOURS, AND NO APPLAUSE, "WASTING" THEIR TAELNTS AND SKILLS AMONG THE POOR AND UNEDUCATED SOMEHOW, THOUGH, IN THE PROCESS OF LOSING THEIR LIVES THEY FIND THEM

LUCKY ARE THE PEACEMAKERS?

THE MOVIE GANDHI CONTAINS A FINE SCENE IN WHICH GANDHI TRIES TO EXPLAIN HIS PRESBYTERIAN MISSIONARY CHARLIE ANDREWS MUMBLES THAT HE DOESN'T THE CITY THE TWO SUDDENLY FIND AT THE MENACING SO SURE. GANDHI REPLIES. "I SUSPECT BLOW, SEVERAL BLOWS TO SHOW AND WHEN YOU DO THAT MAKES HIS HATRED

MARTIN LUTHER KING JR., AGAINST ALL ODDS, AGAINST ALL INSTINCTS OF SELF-PRESERVATION, STAYED TRUE TO THE PRINCIPLE OF PEACEMAKING. HE DID NOT STRIKE BACK.

MAY 3, 1963 17-year-old civil rights demonstrator is attacked by a police dog during protests in Birmingham, Ala.

PHILOSOPHY TO THE

ANDREWS. WALKING TOGETHER IN A SOUTH AFRICAN

THEIR WAY BLOCKED BY YOUNG THUGS. ANDREWS TAKES ONE LOOK

GANGSTERS AND DECIDES TO RUN FOR IT. GANDHI STOPS HIM.

NEW TESTAMENT SAY IF AN ENEMY STRIKES YOU ON THE RIGHT

CHEEK YOU SHOULD OFFER HIM THE LEFT?"

THOUGHT THE PHRASE WAS USED METAPHORICALLY. "I'M NOT

HE MEANT YOU MUST SHOW COURAGE. BE WILLING TO TAKE A

YOU WILL NOT STRIKE BACK NOR WILL YOU BE TURNED ASIDE.

IT CALLS ON SOMETHING IN HUMAN NATURE, SOMETHING THAT

DECREASE AND HIS RESPECT INCREASE."

I NOW VIEW THE BEATITUDES NOT AS PATRONIZING SLOGANS, BUT AS PROFOUND
INSIGHTS INTO THE MYSTERY OF HUMAN EXISTENCE. GOD'S KINGDOM TURNS THE
TABLES UPSIDE DOWN. THE POOR, THE HUNGRY, THE MOURNERS, AND THE OPPRESSED
TRULY ARE BLESSED. NOT BECAUSE OF THEIR MISERABLE STATES, OF COURSE—
JESUS SPENT MUCH OF HIS LIFE TRYING TO REMEDY THOSE MISERIES.

RATHER, THEY ARE BLESSED BECAUSE OF AN INNATE ADVANTAGE THEY HOLD OVER

THOSE MORE COMFORTABLE AND SELF-SUFFICIENT. PEOPLE WHO ARE RICH,

SUCCESSFUL, AND

BEAUTIFUL MAY WELL GO THROUGH LIFE RELYING ON THEIR NATURAL
GIFTS. PEOPLE WHO LACK SUCH NATURAL ADVANTAGES, HENCE
UNDERQUALIFIED FOR SUCCESS IN THE KINGDOM OF THIS WORLD, JUST
MIGHT TURN TO GOD IN THEIR TIME OF NEED.

HUMAN BEINGS DO NOT READILY ADMIT DESPERATION. WHEN THEY DO,

THE KINGDOM OF HEAVEN DRAWS NEAR.

Yet if I care
to listen, I hear a
loud whisper from
the gospel that I did not get
what I deserved. I deserved
punishment and got forgiveness.
I deserved wrath and got love.
I deserved stern lectures and
crawl-on-your-knees repentance;
I got a banquet spread
for me.

From nursery school on we are taught how to succeed in this world. THE EARLY BIRD GETS THE WORM. NO PAIN, NO GAIN. THERE IS NO SUCH THING AS A FREE LUNCH. DEMAND YOUR RIGHTS. I know these rules.

JESUS SAID,

"You're tied down
to the mundane;
I'm in touch with what
is beyond
your horizons.

You live in terms of
what you can   SEE
and TOUCH.

I'm living on other terms."

You're blessed when you
get your inside world, your mind and heart put right.
Then you can see God in the outside
world. "My kingdom," said Jesus, "doesn't consist of
—Jesus   what you see around you. If it did, my followers
would fight so that I wouldn't be handed over to
the Jews. But I'm not that kind of king, not the
world's kind of king."

The gospel of Jesus
is a rogue element
within history, a
demythologizing virus
that will undermine
the false gods of any
culture that would
presume to contain it.

—David Dark

"Jesus thrown everything off balance."
— Flannery O'Connor, Missfit

You're here to be light, bringing out the God-colors in the world.

God is not a secret to be kept.

We're going public with this, as public as a city on a hill. If I make you light-bearers, you don't think I'm going to hide you under a bucket, do you? I'm putting you on a light stand. Now that I've put you there on a hilltop, on a light stand shine! Keep open house; be generous with your lives. By opening up to others, you'll prompt people to open up with God, this generous Father in heaven.

May you believe in God. But may you come to see that
God believes in you. May you have faith in Jesus. But may you come to see
that Jesus has faith that you can be like him. A person of forgiveness, and
peace, and grace, and joy, and hope. And may you be covered in
the dust of your rabbi, Jesus.

—Rob Bell, Dust

You've observed how godless rulers throw their weight around, and when
people get a little power how quickly it goes to their heads. It's not going to
be that way with you. Whoever wants to be great must become a servant.
Whoever wants to be first among you must be your slave. That is what
[I'VE] done: [I] came to serve, not to be served--and then to give away
[my] life in exchange for many who are held hostage.

—JESUS

Jesus reveals
a God who comes in search of us,
a God who
makes room for our freedom even when
it costs the Son's life,
a God who is vulnerable. Above all,
Jesus reveals
a God who is love.

When your eyes are healthy, your whole body
also is full of light. But when they are unhealthy,
your body also is full of darkness.
See to it, then, that the light within you is not darkness.

—JESUS

When I understood that the decision to follow Jesus was very much like the decision the hostages had to make to follow the rescuing Navy SEALS, I knew then that I needed to decide whether or not I would follow Him. The decision was simple once I asked myself, Is Jesus the Son of God, are we being held captive in a world run by Satan, a world filled with brokenness, and do I believe Jesus can rescue me from this condition?

—Donald Miller, Blue Like Jazz

I came into the world
to bring everything into the clear light of
day, making all the distinctions clear,
so that those who have
never seen will see, and those
who have made a great pretense of seeing
will be exposed as blind.

—JESUS

I came so they can have real and eternal life, more and better life than they ever dreamed of.

—JESUS

You're here to be light, bringing out the God-colors in the world. God is not a secret to be kept. Now that I've put you there on a hilltop, on a light stand shine! Keep open house: be generous with your lives.

By opening up to others, you'll prompt people to open up with God, this generous Father in heaven.

—JESUS

The prospect of future rewards in no way cancels out our need to fight for justice now, in this life. Yet it is a plain fact of history that for convicts in the Soviet Gulag and slaves in America and Christians in Roman cages awaiting their turn with the wild beasts, the promise of reward was a source of hope. It keeps you alive. It allows you to believe in a just God after all. Like a bell tolling from another world, Jesus' promise of rewards proc laims that no matter how things appear, there is no future in evil, only in good.

Tony read me this ancient scripture recently that talked about loving either darkness or loving light, and how hard it is to love light and how easy it is to love darkness. I think that is true. Ultimately, we do what we love to do. Because of sin, because I am self-addicted, living in the wreckage of the fall, I am prone to love the things that will kill me. Tony says Jesus gives us the ability to love the things we should love, the things of Heaven.

—Donald Miller, Blue Like Jazz

The apostle Paul boldly called Jesus "the image of the invisible God."

God is, in a word, Christlike. Jesus presents a God with skin on whom we can take or leave, love or ignore.

In this visible, scaled-down model we can discern God's features more

clearly.

If you live wide-eyed in wonder and belief, your body fills up with light. If you live squinty-eyed in greed and distrust, your body is a dank cellar.

The Gospels depict him performing
his first miracle at a wedding,
GIVING PLAYFUL NICKNAMES TO
HIS DISCIPLES, and somehow gaining
a reputation
as a "gluttonous man and a
wine-bibber".

When the pious criticized his disciples for their laxity in spiritual disciplines, Jesus replied, "how can the guests of the bridegroom fast when he is with them?" of all the images he could have chosen for himself, Jesus settled on that of the groom whose radiance cheers up the entire wedding party.

WHEN I ASK A STRANGER. "WHAT IS AN EVANGELICAL CHRISTIAN?" I GET AN ANSWER SOMETHING LIKE THIS: "SOMEONE WHO SUPPORTS FAMILY VALUES AND OPPOSES HOMOSEXUAL RIGHTS AND ABORTION." ☆☆☆☆☆ ☆☆☆☆☆☆ THIS TREND TROUBLES ME BECAUSE THE GOSPEL OF JESUS WAS NOT PRIMARILY A POLITICAL PLATFORM. THE ISSUES THAT CONFRONT CHRISTIANS IN A SECULAR SOCIETY MUST BE FACED AND ADDRESSED AND LEGISLATED, AND A DEMOCRACY GIVES CHRISTIANS EVERY RIGHT TO EXPRESS THEMSELVES. BUT WE DARE NOT INVEST SO MUCH IN THE KINGDOM OF THIS WORLD THAT WE NEGLECT OUR MAIN TASK OF INTRODUCING PEOPLE TO A DIFFERENT KIND OF KINGDOM, ONE BASED SOLELY ON GOD'S GRACE AND FORGIVENESS. PASSING LAWS TO ENFORCE MORALITY SERVES A NECESSARY FUNCTION, TO DAM UP EVIL, BUT IT NEVER SOLVES HUMAN PROBLEMS. IF A CENTURY FROM NOW ALL THAT HISTORIANS CAN SAY ABOUT EVANGELICALS OF THE 2000S IS THAT THEY STOOD FOR FAMILY VALUES, THEN WE WILL HAVE FAILED THE MISSION JESUS GAVE US TO ACCOMPLISH: TO COMMUNICATE GOD'S RECONCILING LOVE TO SINNERS. ☆☆☆☆☆☆☆☆☆☆☆☆☆☆☆☆☆☆ ☆☆☆☆ JESUS DID NOT SAY, "ALL MEN WILL KNOW YOU ARE MY DISCIPLES... IF YOU JUST PASS LAWS, SUPPRESS IMMORALITY, AND RESTORE DECENCY TO FAMILY AND GOVERNMENT," BUT RATHER "... IF YOU LOVE ONE ANOTHER." HE MADE THAT STATEMENT THE NIGHT BEFORE HIS DEATH, A NIGHT WHEN HUMAN POWER, REPRESENTED BY THE MIGHT OF ROME AND THE FULL FORCE OF JEWISH RELIGIOUS AUTHORITIES, COLLIDED HEAD-ON WITH GOD'S POWER. ALL HIS LIFE, JESUS HAD BEEN INVOLVED IN A FORM OF "CULTURE WARS" AGAINST A RIGID RELIGIOUS ESTABLISHMENT AND A PAGAN EMPIRE, YET HE RESPONDED BY GIVING HIS LIFE FOR THOSE WHO OPPOSED HIM. ON THE CROSS, HE FORGAVE THEM. HE HAD COME, ABOVE ALL, TO DEMONSTRATE LOVE: "FOR GOD SO LOVED THE WORLD THAT HE GAVE HIS ONE AND ONLY SON..." ☆☆☆☆☆☆☆☆☆☆☆☆☆☆☆☆☆☆☆☆☆☆☆☆

...daism took the connection between the ...ysical so concretely that those with such ...automatically labeled as "sinners." Thus to ...f blindness or leprosy intrinsically carried the ...itual forgiveness and moral cleansing. With ...e a look at this haunting question that Jesus ...no had been an invalid for thirty-eight years.

When Jesus saw him lying there and learned that he had been in this condition for a long time, he asked him,

"Do you want to get well?"

(JOHN 5:6)

"Do you want to get well? I should think the answer would be rather obvious, but seen through a spiritual lens, as this man perhaps would have, it's anything but rhetorical. I mean,

IF YOU COULD BE HEALED
of LUST
or GREED
or ANGER
or PRIDE
or LYING,
would you really want to?

Just like this crippled man whose identity was defined by his disability, our lives too are arranged around such moral furniture and would look quite different without them. And what if "getting well" spiritually meant a painful amputation of a beloved habit, the denial of a personal passion or the death of a dream? Would you still want to be well? When the patient is our souls and not our bodies, everything changes. The issue is no longer 'Can Jesus heal?' but "Do I want to get well?" – Rick James

I was absolutely thunderstruck by the extraordinary reality of the man I found in the Gospels. I discovered a man who was almost continually frustrated. His frustration leaps out of virtually every page: "What do I have to say to you? How many times do I have to say it? What do I have to do to get through to you?" I also discovered a man who was frequently sad and sometimes depressed, frequently anxious and scared....A man who was terribly, terribly lonely, yet often desperately wanted to be alone. I discovered a man so incredibly real that no one could have made Him up.

It occurred to me then that if the Gospel writers had been into PR and embellishment, as I had assumed, they would have created a Jesus three quarters of Christians still seem to be trying to create...portrayed with a sweet, unending smile on His face, patting little children on the head, just strolling the earth with his unflappable, unshakable equanimity... but the Jesus of the Gospels—who some suggest is the best-kept secret of Christianity—did not have much "peace of mind," as we ordinarily think of peace of mind in the world's terms, and insofar as we can be His followers, perhaps we won't either.

EACHES FROM A BOAT

Sometimes, he was lonely.

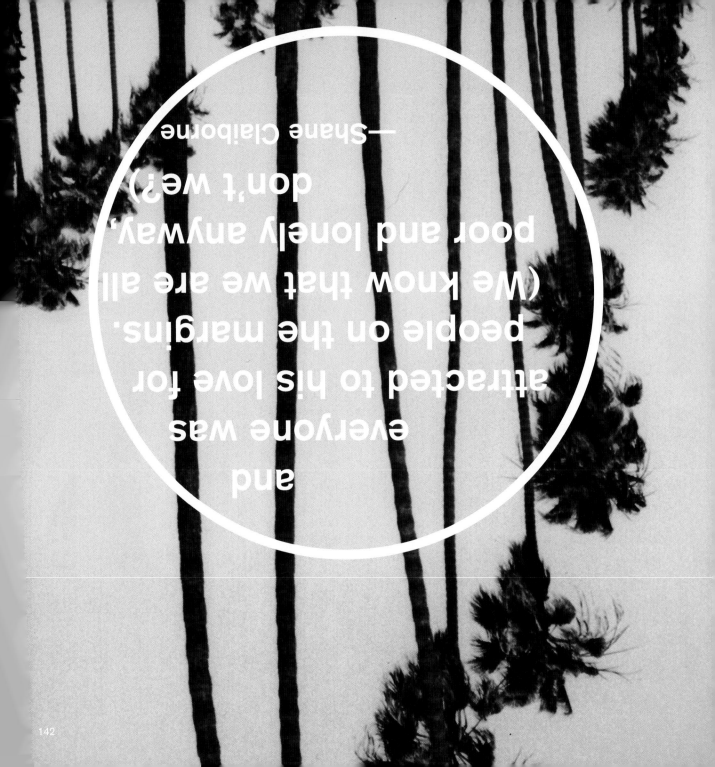

and
everyone was
attracted to his love for
people on the margins.
(We know that we are all
poor and lonely anyway,
don't we?)

—Shane Claiborne

Jesus did not
seek out the rich and
powerful in order to
trickle down his kingdom.
Rather, he joined those
at the bottom, the
outcasts and
undesirables,

As I read John's account, I keep coming back to a peculiar incident that interrupts the progress of the Last Supper. "Jesus knew that the Father had put all things under his power," John begins with a flourish and then adds this incongruous completion: "so he got up from the meal, took off his outer clothing, and **wrapped a towel around his waist.**" In the garb of a slave, he then bent over and washed the grime of Jerusalem from the disciples' feet. What a strange way for the guest of honor to act during a final meal with his friends. What incomprehensible behavior from a ruler who would momentarily announce, "I confer on you a kingdom." In those days, foot washing was considered so degrading that a master could not require it of a Jewish slave. The scene of the foot washing stands out to author M. Scott Peck as one of the most significant events of Jesus' life. "Until that moment the whole point of things had been for someone to get on top, and once he had gotten on top to stay on top or else attempt to get farther up. But here this man already on top—who was rabbi, teacher, master— suddenly got

down on the bottom. and began to wash the feet of his followers. In that one act Jesus symbolically overturned the whole social order. Hardly comprehending what was happening, even his own disciples were almost horrified by his behavior." Later that same evening a dispute arose among the disciples as to which of them was considered to be greatest. Pointedly, Jesus did not deny the human instinct of competition and ambition. He simply redirected it: "the greatest among you should be like the youngest, and the one who rules like the one who serves." That is when he proclaimed, "I confer on you a kingdom"—a kingdom, in other words, based on service and humility. In the foot washing, the disciples had seen a living tableau of what he meant. Following that example has not gotten any easier in two thousand years.

Jews in Jesus' day envisioned a ladder reaching higher and higher towards God, a hierarchy expressed in the very architecture of the temple. Gentiles and "half-breeds" like the Samaritans were permitted only in the outer Court of the Gentiles; a wall separated them from the next partition, which admitted Jewish women. Jewish men could proceed one stage further, but only priests could enter the sacred areas. Finally, only one priest, the high priest, could enter the Most Holy Place, and that just once a year on the day of Yom Kippur. The society was, in effect, a religious caste system based on steps toward holiness, and the Pharisees' scrupulosity reinforced the system daily. All their rules on washing hands and avoiding defilement were an attempt to make themselves acceptable to God. Had not God set forth lists of desirable (spotless) and undesirable (flawed, unclean) animals for use in sacrifice? Had not God banned sinners, menstruating women, the physically deformed, and other "undesirables" from the temple? The Qumram community of the Essenes made a firm rule, "No madman, or lunatic, or simpleton, or fool, no blind man, or maimed, or lame, or deaf man, and no minor, shall enter into the Community." In the midst of this religious caste system, Jesus appeared. To the Pharisees' dismay he had no qualms about socializing with children or sinners or even Samaritans. He touched, or was touched by, the "unclean": those with leprosy, the deformed, a hemorrhaging woman, the lunatic and possessed. Although Levitical laws prescribed a day of purification after touching a sick person, Jesus conducted mass healings in which he touched scores of sick people; he never concerned himself with the rules of defilement after contact with the sick or even the dead. To take just one example of the revolutionary changes Jesus set in motion, consider Jesus' attitude toward women. In those days, at every synagogue service Jewish men prayed, "Blessed art thou, O Lord, who hast not made me a woman." Women sat in a separate section, were not counted in quorums, and were rarely taught the Torah. In social life, few women would talk to men outside of their families, and a woman was to touch no man but her spouse. Yet Jesus associated freely with women and taught some as his disciples. A Samaritan woman who had been through five husbands, Jesus tapped to lead a spiritual revival (notably, he began the conversation by asking her for help). A prostitute's anointing, he accepted with gratitude. Women traveled with his band of followers, no doubt stirring up much gossip. Women populated Jesus' parables and illustrations, and frequently he did miracles on their behalf. According to biblical scholar Walter Wink, Jesus violated the mores of his time in every single encounter with women recorded in the four Gospels. Truly, as Paul would later say, in Christ "There is neither Jew nor Greek, slave nor free, male nor female. . . . " Indeed, for women and other oppressed people, Jesus turned upside down the accepted wisdom of the day. Pharisees believed that touching an unclean person polluted the one who touched. But when Jesus touched a person with leprosy, Jesus did not become soiled—the leprous became clean. When an immoral woman washed Jesus' feet, she went away forgiven and transformed. When he defied custom to enter a pagan's house, the pagan's servant was healed. In word and in deed Jesus was proclaiming a radically new gospel of grace: to get clean a person did not have to journey to Jerusalem, offer sacrifices, and undergo purification rituals. All a person had to do was follow Jesus. As Walter Wink puts it, "The contagion of holiness overcomes the contagion of uncleanness." In short, Jesus moved the emphasis from God's holiness (exclusive) to God's mercy (inclusive). Instead of the message "No undesirables allowed," he proclaimed, "In God's kingdom there are no undesirables."

WER
V

The more I get to know Jesus, the more impressed I am by "the miracle of restraint." The miracles Satan suggested, the signs and wonders the Pharisees demanded, the final proofs I yearn for–these would offer no serious obstacle to an omnipotent God. More amazing is his refusal to perform and overwhelm. God's terrible insistence on human freedom is so absolute that he granted us the power to live as though he did not exist, to spit in his face, to crucify him. I believe God insists on such restraint because no pyrotechnic displays of omnipotence

LOVE

will achieve the response he desires. Although power can force obedience, only love can summon a response of love, which is the one thing God wants from us and the reason he created us.

LOVE

The crowd at Jesus' crucifixion challenged him to prove himself by climbing down from the cross, but not one person thought of what actually would happen: that he would die and then come back. Once the scenario played out, though, to those who knew Jesus best it made perfect sense. The style fit God's pattern and character. God has always chosen the slow and difficult way, respecting human freedom regardless of cost. "God did not abolish the fact of evil: He transformed it," wrote Dorothy Sayers. "He did not stop the crucifixion: He rose from the dead." The hero bore all consequences, yet somehow triumphed.

I believe in the Resurrection primarily because I have gotten to know God. I know that God is love, and I also know that we human beings want to keep alive those whom we love. For whatever reason—human freedom lies at the core, I imagine— God allows a planet where a man dies scuba diving in the prime of life and a woman dies in a fiery crash on the way to a church missions conference. But I believe—if I did not believe this, I would not believe in a loving God—that God is not satisfied with such a blighted planet. Divine love will find a way to overcome. God will not let death win.

One detail in the Easter stories has always intrigued me: Why did Jesus keep the scars from his crucifixion? Presumably he could have had any resurrected body he wanted, and yet he chose one identifiable mainly by scars that could be seen and touched. Why?

I believe the story of Easter would be incomplete without those scars on the hands, the feet, and the side of Jesus. When human beings fantasize, we dream of pearly straight teeth and wrinkle-free skin and sexy ideal shapes. We dream of an unnatural state: the perfect body. But for Jesus, being confined in a skeleton and human skin was the unnatural state. The scars are, to him, an emblem of life on our planet, a permanent reminder of those days of confinement and suffering.

I take hope in Jesus' scars. From the perspective of heaven, they represent the most horrible event that has ever happened in the history of the universe. Even that event, though—the crucifixion— Easter turned into a memory. Because of Easter, I can hope that the tears we shed, the blows we receive, the emotional pain, the heartache over lost friends and loved ones, all these will become memories, like Jesus' scars. Scars never completely go away, but neither do they hurt any longer. We will have re-created bodies, a re-created heaven and earth. We will have a new start, an Easter start.

Easter hits a new note of hope and faith that what God did once in a graveyard in Jerusalem, he can and will repeat on grand scale.

Against all odds,

the irrevers-ible will be reversed.

For us.

For the world.

153

The Bible from Genesis 3 to Rev

God reckless with desire to get

decisive blow of reconciliation

journey to planet earth. The Bible's

the family united once again.

elation 22 tells the story of a

his family back. God struck the

when he sent the Son on the long

last scene ends in jubilation,

CAMBODIAN girl reunited with her father in camp for displaced persons.

God didn't go to all
the trouble of sending
his Son merely to point an
accusing finger, telling the
world how bad it was. He
came to help, to put the
world right again.

—Jesus (John 3:16-17)

This is how
much God loved
the world: He gave his
Son, his one and only Son.
And this is why: so that no
one need be destroyed; by
believing in him, anyone
can have a whole and
lasting life.

SPECIAL THANKS TO JON ARNOLD, RICK JAMES, JOHN TOPLIFF AND KURT WILSON FOR THEIR
INVALUABLE FEEDBACK THROUGHOUT THE CREATIVE PROCESS.

visualjesusbook.com